THE ADV...

Captain Pugwash

BEST PIRATE
JOKES

THE ADVENTURES OF
Captain Pugwash ™

BEST PIRATE
JOKES

Ian D. Rylett

RED
FOX

With special thanks to Andy Rigg,
horder of alarming ties
and devout Pugwash fanatic

A Red Fox Book

Published by Random House Children's Books
20 Vauxhall Bridge Road, London SW1V 2SA

A division of The Random House Group Ltd
London Melbourne Sydney Auckland
Johannesburg and agencies throughout the world

The Adventures of Captain Pugwash
Created by John Ryan
© Britt Allcroft (Development Ltd) Limited 2000
All rights worldwide Britt Allcroft (Development Ltd) Limited
CAPTAIN PUGWASH is a trademark of Britt Allcroft (Development Ltd) Limited
THE BRITT ALLCROFT COMPANY is a trademark
of The Britt Allcroft Company plc

Illustrations by Ian Hillyard

1 3 5 7 9 10 8 6 4 2

Printed and bound in Great Britain by Cox and Wyman Ltd

THE RANDOM HOUSE GROUP Limited Reg. No. 954009

www.randomhouse.co.uk

ISBN 0 09 941319 1

Contents

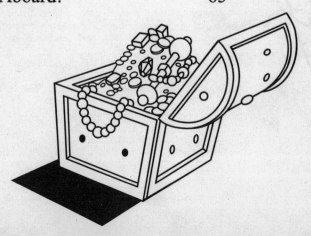

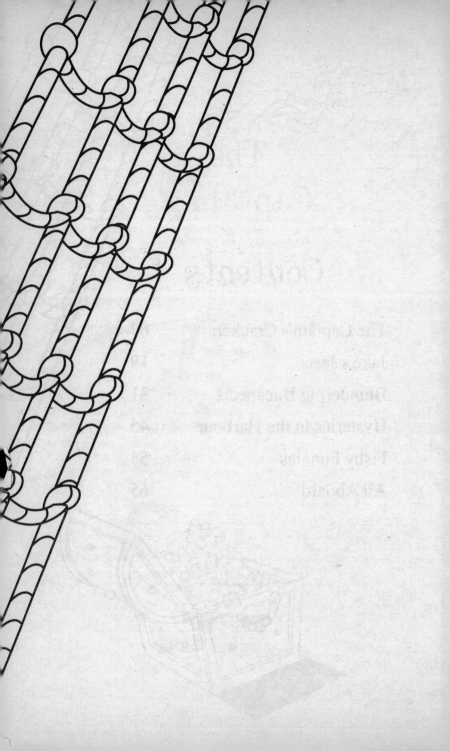

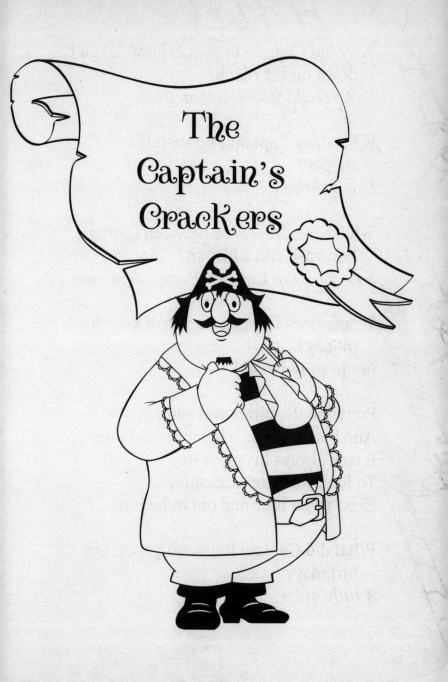

The Captain's Crackers

Why did Captain Pugwash jump up and
    down on the plank?
So he could spring into action.

What does Captain Pugwash like for
    supper?
Lamb cutlass.

What's the difference between Captain
    Pugwash and a biscuit?
You can't dip Captain Pugwash in your tea.

Where does Captain Pugwash keep his
    money?
In the sand bank.

Pugwash the pirate was plump,
And his crewmates he never did thump.
It was always his pleasure,
To look for Jake's treasure,
Even when it turned out to be junk.

What did Captain Pugwash get on his
    birthday?
A little older.

How can you tell if Captain Pugwash is
    hiding in your fridge?
The door won't close.

Why does Captain Pugwash live on a ship?
Because houses won't float.

How does Captain Pugwash dress on a cold day?
Quickly.

Where was Captain Pugwash when his candle blew out?
In the dark.

Why didn't Captain Pugwash believe what the sardine said?
Because it sounded fishy.

Why did Captain Pugwash persuade a footballer to join his crew?
Because he heard he could tackle anything.

Why did Captain Pugwash take up sword dancing?
Because it seemed a fun way to cut his toenails.

Did you hear Jonah's joke about the smelly pirate?
Never mind, it stinks!

How do you tell the difference between Captain Pugwash and a tin of chicken soup?
Read the label.

Why did Captain Pugwash go to bed?
Because the bed wouldn't go to him.

When is Captain Pugwash like a plank of wood?
When he's aboard.

What did Captain Pugwash call his
  girlfriend?
My little treasure.

What does the ocean say when it sees
  Captain Pugwash?
Nothing, it just waves.

Why did Captain Pugwash go to the barber
  to have his head shaved?
*Because he couldn't stand his hair any
  longer.*

What type of hat does Captain Pugwash
  wear when it's raining?
A wet one.

Why wouldn't Captain Pugwash touch the
  ship's log?
*Because he kept getting splinters in his
  hands.*

What's the last thing Captain Pugwash takes
  off before he goes to bed?
His feet off the floor.

Why did Captain Pugwash cut the legs off
  his bed?
Because he wanted to lie low for a while.

When does Captain Pugwash weigh as
  much as a sardine?
When the scales are broken.

CAPTAIN PUGWASH: Weigh anchor!
WILLY: Six stone, seven pounds.

On what side of the Black Pig does the
   anchor hang?
On the outside.

WILLY: What's your parrot's name?
JONAH: I don't know – he won't tell me.

JONAH: I've just swallowed my tankard.
TOM: Are you choking?
JONAH: No – I really did!

If Pugwash the pirate promptly pushed Jake
off the plank, how many P's in that?
None – there are no P's in 'that'.

What happened when Willy rested on the
plank?
He soon dropped off!

Can Willy jump higher than a lamp post?
Yes – lamp posts can't jump.

What's the difference between the crew of
the Black Pig and a piece of string for
your shoe?
*One chases the loot, the other laces the
boot.*

How do you stop Willy charging?
Confiscate his credit card.

Why does the crew of the Black Pig wear
   big boots?
Because of their amazing feats.

What do you get if you cross Willy's brain
   with a piece of elastic?
A stretch of the imagination.

TOM: I'm afraid the ship's sinking, Captain.
CAPTAIN PUGWASH: Quick, bring me a
   bar of soap.
TOM: A bar of soap?
CAPTAIN PUGWASH: Yes – it'll help me
   wash.

TOM: They say Cut-throat Jake has a good
   head on his shoulders.
MR MATE: Yes – it's a pity it isn't on his
   neck.

WILLY: Why do you keep looking at the
   clock?
MR MATE: That's not a clock, it's a
   compass.

MR MATE: I was shipwrecked once and had to live for a week on a tin of pilchards.

WILLY: Gracious me, I'm surprised you didn't fall off.

What happened when Willy decided to get himself a pen pal?

He ended up writing to a pig.

WILLY: I hear Captain Pugwash is very
     musical.
MR MATE: Yes – he's always fiddling with
     his beard.

Recommended reading: *Pugwash's
Treasure* by Ivor Fortune.

What fur do you get from Cut-throat Jake?
As fur away as possible.

Why does Cut-throat Jake carry a sword?
Because swords can't walk.

What game do Cut-throat Jake's crew play
  in water?
Swimming pool.

What do you give Cut-throat Jake when he's
  sick?
Lots of room.

What do you call Cut-throat Jake when he
has two gold baubles in his ears?
*Anything you like because he won't be able
to hear you.*

What should you do if Cut-throat Jake
borrows your pen?
Wait until he gives it back.

What's big, fat and smells?
Cut-throat Jake's bottom.

What's the quickest way to escape from Cut-
throat Jake?
Run.

There was a dark pirate called Jake,
Who saw treasure he thought he could take.
He had a big tool,
To prise out the jewel.
Unfortunately it was only a fake!

How many pirates does it take to fill the
Flying Dustman?
Just one – after that it's no longer empty.

When Cut-throat Jake hijacked a treasure ship, the captain refused to tell him where the treasure was hidden. All he did was ramble around the subject – until Cut-throat Jake drew his sword. He soon got to the point.

How many of Cut-throat Jake's crew does it take to make the Flying Dustman smelly?
Just a phew.

What do you get if you cross Jake with a comedian?
Something that keeps trying to joke people to death.

Knock, knock.
Who's there?
Doughnut.
Doughnut who?
Doughnut look now, Cut-throat Jake's coming.

What's the best way to talk to Stinka?
Long distance.

Who went aboard Cut-throat Jake's ship and
   lived to tell the tale?
Cut-throat Jake.

I hear Cut-throat Jake is so tough he uses
   barbed wire for dental floss.

SWINE: I expect it's terribly difficult
   getting milk aboard the Flying Dustman.
DOOK: Yes, that's why I bought myself a
   cow.
SWINE: Well, there's nothing like taking
   things into your own hands.

Why should you never listen to Dook in bed?
Because he's lying.

STINKA: Should you eat chips with your fingers?
SWINE: No – fingers should be eaten separately.

DOOK: My parrot lays square eggs.
SWINE: That's amazing! Does she speak, too?
DOOK: Yes, but she only says one word.
SWINE: What's that?
DOOK: Ouch!

What happened when Stinka robbed the treasure ship?
The coastguard was soon on the scent.

What are long, black and incredibly smelly?
Cut-throat Jake's toenails.

Why is Cut-throat Jake so strong?
Because he holds up ships.

SWINE: What did Cut-throat Jake say when his new ship sank?
STINKA: Shall I leave out all the swear words?
SWINE: Yes.
STINKA: He didn't say a word.

What do you get if you cross Cut-throat Jake's socks with a boomerang?
A terrible smell that you can't get rid of.

What should you do if you find Swine in
  your bed?
Sleep somewhere else.

Does Dook snore?
Only when he's asleep.

What do you get if you cross Cut-throat
  Jake with a boy scout?
*Someone who frightens old ladies across
  the road.*

Then there was the time Dook wrote to the
lonely hearts club.
*They wrote back saying they weren't that
lonely!*

CUT-THROAT JAKE: Doctor, Doctor, no
one likes me because I'm a pirate.
DOCTOR: Next!

What does Cut-throat Jake grow if he fights
long enough?
Tired.

FEMALE PRISONER (after walking the
plank): Help! There's a shark coming.
DOOK: Don't worry, it's only a man-eater.

What did Cut-throat Jake get for Christmas?
Fat.

What did the hostage say when Swine fell
overboard?
Nothing.

How do you stop Stinka smelling?
Put a peg on his nose.

What do you call Cut-throat Jake when he's in a bad mood?
Sir.

What do you get if you cross Cut-throat Jake with a crustacean?
A smash and crab raid.

Knock, knock.
Who's there?
Luke.
Luke who?
Luke out, Cut-throat Jake's coming!

Have you heard the joke about the time Swine couldn't stop burping?
Never mind – it's not worth repeating.

What steps should you take if you're being followed by Cut-throat Jake?
Big ones.

'Help!' cried the man, moments after walking the plank. 'A shark's just bitten my leg off!'

'Which one?' asked Stinka.

'How would I know?' the man replied. 'All sharks look the same to me!'

What's Cut-throat Jake's favourite instrument?
The loot.

Why couldn't Dook, Swine and Stinka play cards aboard the Flying Dustman?
Because Cut-throat Jake sat on the deck.

Recommended reading: Who Stole Cut-throat Jake's Treasure? by M. T. Chest.

Recommended reading: *Cut-throat Jake* by Robin Ships.

Recommended reading: *The Trial of Cut-throat Jake* by Freda Pirate.

Blundering
Bucaneers

What did the coastguard say when he saw a
gang of pirates running towards him?
Look, here come the pirates.

What did the coastguard say when he saw a
gang of pirates running towards him with
sunglasses on?
Nothing – he didn't recognise them.

How do you get a one-armed pirate out of
the rigging?
By waving to him.

Knock, knock.
Who's there?
Colleen.
Colleen who?
Colleen this deck or you'll walk the plank!

What's the difference between a pirate's flag and a fat runner?
One's a Jolly Roger, the other's a jolly jogger.

Which pirate had the warmest bottom?
Long John Silver.

Then there was the old pirate who went deaf.
All his friends clubbed together and bought him a herring aid.

What do you get if you cross a whale with a flying fish?
Flat pirates.

What type of ships do clever pirates study?
Scholarships.

Why was the pirate glad that everyone
  called him Stinka?
Because that was his name.

Knock, knock.
Who's there?
Andy.
Andy who?
Andy me leg back,
I keep falling over!

Did you hear about the fat pirate?
The rest of the crew had to give him a wide berth.

Did you hear about the idiot pirate?
He thought a blood vessel was a new type of ship.

Why do pirates wear glasses?
So they don't bump into other pirates.

What does a one-legged pirate fear the most?
Woodworm.

What type of pirate never steals?
A dead one.

What do you call a pirate who doesn't have all his fingers on one hand?
Normal. Fingers are supposed to be on both hands.

What has fifty patches and fifty swords?
Fifty pirates.

What does a miserable pirate do when he's
    short of money?
He takes in a jolly lodger.

What do you call a good-looking, friendly
    pirate?
A failure.

Why did the bald pirate climb into the
    rigging?
To get some fresh 'air.

What sits at the bottom of the sea and
    makes pirates offers they can't refuse?
The Cod Father.

Why do pirates always stick together?
Because they don't bath often enough.

What's Greybeard the pirate's middle name?
The.

Why did the irate sailor go for a pee?
Because he wanted to be a pirate.

Knock, knock.
Who's there?
Bet.
Bet who?
Bet you've never met a real pirate before.

What do you call a happy, one-legged
   pirate?
An hoptimist.

How can you tell if a pirate has a glass eye?
It usually comes out in the conversation.

Which pirate had the biggest hat?
The one with the biggest head.

Knock, knock.
Who's there?
Guv.
Guv who?
Guv us me cutlass back!

Knock, knock.
Who's there?
Fanny.
Fanny who?
Fanny the way people don't like pirates.

Knock, knock.
Who's there?
Anna.
Anna who?
Another pirate, that's who!

PIRATE CAPTAIN (to galley slaves): I've decided to go water-skiing . . .

What did the pirate do when he lost his hand?
He went to the second-hand shop.

Why do crazy pirates eat biscuits?
Because they're crackers.

How do you make a slow pirate fast?
Don't feed him for a fortnight.

Knock, knock.
Who's there.
Howard.
Howard who?
Howard you like to walk the plank?

What do you get if you cross a pirate with
a dustman?
Organised grime.

What's mean, ugly and green?
A seasick pirate.

How do you recognise a stupid pirate?
He's the one with a patch over his good eye.

What's the hottest part of a pirate's face?
His sideburns.

What do you call a pirate who's written a
   book?
An author.

What do you call a married pirate with nine
   children?
Tired.

What happened when the pirate ship sank in
   shark-infested waters?
It came back with a skeleton crew.

Did you hear about the pirate who went for
   a swim?
Something he disagreed with ate him.

What's incredibly mean and wanders around
   the desert?
A lost pirate.

What's incredibly mean and covered in
  safety pins?
A punk pirate.

Why did the pirate wear a three-cornered
  hat?
Because their bowler was at the cleaners.

Where do mean, bad-tempered pirates live?
In a far distant terror-tory.

What happened when the pirate couldn't tell
  the difference between tar and treacle?
Their ship sank.

When do pirates have four feet?
When there are two of them.

How do you make a thin pirate fat?
*Throw them out of the rigging and they'll
  come down 'plump'.*

What do you give a pirate who's got
  everything?
Penicillin.

Knock, knock.
Who's there?
Max.
Max who?
Max no difference, you're still going to
  walk the plank.

What should you do if you're being
  followed by a pirate?
*Hope they're on their way to a fancy dress
  party.*

What has three eyes and goes, 'Glub, glub,
  glub'?
Three one-eyed pirates on a sinking ship.

Why did the pirate visit the psychiatrist?
Because he thought everyone liked him.

What's incredibly mean and travels at
  70 m.p.h.?
A pirate in a power boat.

Why do pirates usually look drunk?
Because they're generally half legless.

'My daughter's just married a pirate'
'Oh, really?'
'No, O'Reilly'

Why did the pirate's parrot fly over the
  racecourse?
Because he fancied a flutter on the horses.

Why did the pirate visit the psychiatrist?
Because he thought everyone liked him.

Recommended reading: *The Unpunctual
Pirate by Mr Ship*.

Hysterics
in the
Harbour

There was a young lad from Portobello,
Who thought he could sail on a cello.
He wasn't too bright,
But, oh what a site,
To see such a wet, soggy fellow.

WILLY: This parrot you sold me hasn't said
a single word, and you promised me it
would repeat everything it heard.
ROOK: So it would, only it's stone deaf.

Knock, knock.
Who's there?
Lettuce.
Lettuce who?
Lettuce in, Scratchwood's coming!

Knock, knock.
Who's there?
One.
One who?
One-der where the treasure's hidden.

GOVERNOR: Having heard the evidence I have decided to give you a suspended sentence.
PIRATE: Thank you.
GOVERNOR: Don't thank me, you're going to be hanged.

GOVERNOR: How do you plead? Guilty or not guilty?
PIRATE: I can't say until I've heard the evidence.

Knock, knock.
Who's there?
Police.
Police who?
Police let me in – the Governor's coming!

MR MATE: I hear Scratchwood is looking
for a pirate with one eye called
Greybeard.
WILLY: What's his other eye called?

ROOK: I've just got a parrot for my wife.
TOM: Wow – what a swap!

MR MATE: I've got a three-mile swim
across the harbour to get home tonight.
JONAH: Why don't you take the ferry?
MR MATE: I did once, but the coastguard
made me give it back.

There was an old pirate called Flapp.
It's said Pugwash gave him a map.
He took it with pleasure,
Discovered the treasure,
And now he's a wealthy old chap.

GOVERNOR: I can't stand the sun, it's driving me mad.
SCRATCHWOOD: Well, why don't you try the *Times*?

Knock, knock.
Who's there?
Ivor.
Ivor who?
Ivor lost the treasure map!

What happened to the pirate who ran away
  with the Governor?
The police made him bring him back.

Knock, knock.
Who's there?
Bet.
Bet who?
Bet I know where the treasure's hidden.

TEACHER: This essay on the Pacific is
  word for word the same as your brother's.
PUPIL: I know, sir – it's the same ocean.

Who has a parrot that shouts, 'Pieces of
  four!'?
Short John Silver.

Knock, knock.
Who's there?
Owl.
Owl who?
Owl you find the treasure without the map?

Why did Willy buy a packet of birdseed?
Because he wanted to grow himself a parrot.

Knock, knock.
Who's there?
Jimmy.
Jimmy who?
Jimmy the money and I'll leave you alone.

CAPTAIN PUGWASH: Right, today we're
  going to Cutlass Island to collect our
  treasure.
MR MATE: But you said it was full of
  lions. They might eat us!
CAPTAIN PUGWASH: Don't worry,
  they're only dandelions.

TOM: What did you get your mother for
  Christmas?
ROOK: I bought her a parrot that can talk
  fifteen languages.
TOM: Really? What did she think of it?
ROOK: She said it was delicious.

Knock, knock.
Who's there?
Arfur.
Arfur who?
Arfur got where the treasure map is.

Knock, knock.
Who's there?
Juno.
Juno who?
Juno where the treasure's hidden?

There was a little fellow,
From nearby Portobello.
He was rather thin,
With a very big chin,
And his wooden leg turned out to be hollow.

Knock, knock.
Who's there?
Hugo.
Hugo who?
Hugo fetch the treasure.

PIRATE: Doctor, Doctor, my wooden leg
    keeps giving me terrible headaches.
DOCTOR: How is that?
PIRATE: When I get home from the tavern
    my wife hits me over the head with it.

Recommended reading: *The Shipwrecked
Pirate* by I. Malone.

Fishy
Funnies

Which fish has the lowest voice?
A bass.

What's the difference between a fish and a piano?
You can't tuna fish.

What happened to the shark who ate an octopus?
He was armed to the teeth.

Which fish is famous?
A starfish.

What type of house weighs the least?
A lighthouse.

What do you call a baby crab?
A little nipper.

Why was the crab arrested?
Because he was always pinching things.

Which fish is musical?
A piano tuna.

Why did the ocean roar?
Wouldn't you if you had crabs on your bottom?

What's the fastest fish around?
A motorpike.

Which sea creature can add?
An octoplus.

What do you get if you cross a whale with a duckling?
Moby Duck.

Which fish always go to heaven?
Angel fish.

How do fish go into business?
They start on a small scale.

What type of cat lives in the ocean?
An octopus.

Why is it easy to weigh a fish?
Because they have their own scales.

What lives in the sea and goes, 'Dot, dot, dash'?
A morse cod.

What lives at the bottom of the sea and wobbles?
A jellyfish.

What sits at the bottom of the sea and trembles?
A nervous wreck.

What kind of fish performs operations?
A sturgeon.

Knock, knock.
Who's there?
Tina.
Tina who?
Tina sardines.

What did the boy octopus say to the girl octopus?
I want to hold your hand hand hand hand hand hand hand hand.

What weighs more – a pound of whales or a
    pound of sardines?
Neither – they both weigh the same.

What advice did the mother fish give to stop
    her baby being caught?
Don't fall for any old lines.

Did you hear about the crazy pirate who
    drove his car into the sea?
He was trying to dip his headlights.

What's a mermaid?
A deep she-fish.

BABY SARDINE (looking at a submarine):
    Mummy, Mummy, what's that?
MOTHER SARDINE: Don't worry, it's only
    a tin of people.

How do you get a shellfish up a cliff?
Oyster up.

Why did the lobster blush?
Because the seaweed.

How did the ten ton whale feel when he lost
    a ton?
Delighted.

What's a sea monster's favourite food?
Fish and ships.

What sits at the bottom of the sea and
    terrorises mermaids?
Jack the kipper.

What sea creature has to have a reason for
    doing anything?
A porpoise.

What can run but can't walk?
Water.

What does a deep sea diver get paid when
he works extra hours?
Undertime.

What do you get if you cross a whale with a
nun?
Blubber and sister.

What's worse than a whale with indigestion?
A turtle with claustrophobia.

SERGEANT: What's your name?
RECRUIT: Fish, sir.
SERGEANT: OK, you can serve in the tank.

What leaves footprints on the sea bed?
A sole.

Why is fishing like measles?
Because it's catching.

TEACHER: What family does the whale
  belong to?
PUPIL: I don't know, Miss. Nobody in our
  street has one.

CUSTOMER IN PET SHOP: This goldfish
  you sold me is always asleep.
SHOP ASSISTANT: That's not a goldfish,
  it's a kipper.

What does an electric eel taste like?
Shocking.

Why did the vicar hire an aqualung?
Because he was interested in saving soles.

Where do you weigh a whale?
At a whale-weigh station.

Why are so many people mad about fishing?
Because it's an easy thing to get hooked on.

Recommended reading: *Sea Fishing* by
Adolph Fynn.

When is the Black Pig not the Black Pig?
When it turns into a harbour.

STINKA: There goes six bells. It's my
watch below.
PRISONER: My, what a loud watch you
must have.

Knock, knock.
Who's there?
Eye.
Eye who?
Eye-eye, Captain!

TOM: You are invited to dine at the
Captain's table, your duchess-ship.
DUCHESS: Dine with the Captain? I spend
all this money to go to Rumbaba and you
expect me to eat with the crew!

Knock, knock.
Who's there?
Harry.
Harry who?
Harry up, the boat's sinking!

DUCHESS: Boy, I wish to complain about the washing machine in my cabin.

TOM: Washing machine?

DUCHESS: Yes, every time I put my clothes in it, they disappear.

TOM: That's not a washing machine – that's a porthole!

What bus sailed the seven seas?
Columbus.

If there are ten cats on the Black Pig and
   one jumps overboard, how many will
   be left?
None, because they're all copycats.

What did Stinka say when he saw a fat lady
   aboard ship?
A vast behind!

'And here,' said Tom, pointing at a brass plate on the deck, 'is where the gallant Captain fell.'

'I'm not surprised,' replied the Duchess. 'I nearly tripped over it myself.'

When is a boat the cheapest?
When it's a sail boat.

PASSENGER: Why is this station called Fish Hook?
PORTER: Because it's at the end of the line.

How far can the Flying Dustman travel in one day?
Twenty miles to the galleon.

What vegetable is dangerous aboard the Black Pig?
A leek.

Why is the Pacific like a pirate with an idea?
Because it's just a notion.

Knock, knock.
Who's there?
Kipper.
Kipper who?
Kipper your mouth shut and your hands on
the oars.

BOY: Being a ship's carpenter must be
really easy.
CARPENTER: Yes, it's just plane sailing.

What's the difference between a pirate ship
and someone who hates bad weather?
*One roams in the main, the other moans in
the rain.*

Why do pirates in a crow's nest never
disagree?
Because they don't want to fall out.

Knock, knock.
Who's there?
Jethro.
Jethro who?
Jethro the boat and stop talking.

PRISONER: How many people work on this ship?
SWINE: Oh, about half of them.

PRISONER: This cabin isn't fit for pigs!
CUT-THROAT JAKE: Well, the swine before you didn't complain.

On which ship did the first insects sail to
    America?
The Mayfly.

What's the hardest part about learning to
    climb the rigging?
The deck.

How does the Black Pig show its affection?
It hugs the shore.

Knock, knock.
Who's there.
Halibut.
Halibut who?
Halibut letting me aboard?

Doctor, Doctor, people keep throwing me in
    the sea.
Don't talk wet.

Who's the biggest gangster in the sea?
Al Caprawn.

Knock, knock.
Who's there?
Jaws.
Jaws who?
Jaws Truly.

When the pirate captain died he wanted to be buried at sea. Unfortunately the two idiot pirates given the job nearly drowned while digging the hole!

Who was the strongest man in the Bible?
Jonah – even the whale couldn't keep him down.

What's black, floats on the sea and whispers 'Panties'?
Refined oil.

What's black, floats on the sea and shouts 'Knickers!'?
Crude oil.

What musical instrument from Spain helps
  you to fish?
A castanet.

What happens if you throw a blue hat in the
  Red Sea?
It gets wet.

What goes in to the sea pink and comes out blue?
A swimmer in January.

SIMON: Dad, where's the Pacific?
FATHER: Ask your mother, she's always moving things.

HOSTAGE: How often do galleons like this sink?
DOOK: Only once.

Two galleons sank. One was carrying red paint, the other was carrying purple paint. The pirates are now marooned.

What doesn't get any wetter no matter how much it rains?
The ocean.

What children live in the ocean?
Life buoys.

Recommended reading: *Pirate-infested Waters* by B. Warned.

75

Recommended reading: *Walking The Plank* by I. C. Water.

Recommended reading: *In The Crow's Nest* by Luke Out.

Knock, knock.
Who's there?
Seas.
Seas who?
Seas you later, shipmates, because that's the end of the book!

Join Captain Pugwash on another swashbuckling adventure!

The Portobello Plague

When the crew of the Black Pig arrive in Portobello harbour they hear a strange voice warning them there's a plague on shore. Stranded on their ship with no food, Pugwash hatches a plan to feed his crew.

ISBN 0 09 940822 8

£2.99

THE ADVENTURES OF

Captain Pugwash

Join Captain Pugwash on another swashbuckling adventure!

The Double-dealing Duchess

Captain Pugwash accepts a paying passenger who is not all she seems. Pugwash is blinded by money, but Tom smells a rat. Will he be able to unveil the true identity of this double-dealing duchess before it's too late for the Captain…?

ISBN 0 09 940819 8

£2.99